John was happily walking home after school. His friends had already left, so he was walking alone.

However, the road ahead was blocked by large trucks clearing branches.
"How can I get home if I can't pass through here?" John worried.

To the side, there was a flower bed, but John was afraid of being attacked by bees if he went that way.
Feeling overwhelmed, he began to cry.

"Hey, kid, what's wrong?"
a man passing by asked.
"I need to get home, but the road is blocked. I'm scared to go through the flower bed."
"Well then, let me help you. Hold my hand," the man offered.

"Thank you." As they approached the trucks, John noticed there was a path that people could use to pass through.
"Oh, there was a way through! I didn't see it from a distance. I'm so embarrassed."

The man smiled and said,
"It's okay. I'm scared of bees too. But with you by my side, I could get closer and see that it wasn't such a big problem. You helped me, John. Now, I've learned that a big problem from afar might have a solution up close. Thank you, John."
"Thank you, sir." John smiled as he headed home.

When John got home, he started preparing for a presentation the next day.
But the more he thought about it, the more scared he felt about speaking in front of his classmates.

"I have a presentation tomorrow, and I'm scared to talk in front of so many people."

"That's understandable. It can be scary if you're not used to it. Let's practice so you can do well. The more you practice, the more comfortable you'll become."
John practiced hard in front of his family.

On the day of the presentation, John was nervous, but he spoke confidently to his classmates, just as he had practiced.

"It's already over. It wasn't as bad as I feared," he thought. John felt great.

When he got home, he wrote in his diary about the blocked road and the presentation.
He thought about the things he had feared and went to his dad for advice.

"Dad, am I a coward?"
John shared his concerns about the blocked road and the presentation.

His dad smiled and said,
"John, everyone feels fear sometimes. Fear helps us. When the road was blocked, you were lucky it worked out, but it could have been a problem. Asking for help was the right thing to do. And remember, even if something looks scary from afar, a closer look can reveal a solution.

It's the same with the presentation. The reason you were able to do well was that fear told you to practice. Anyone would be scared to speak in front of a crowd, but with enough practice, what happened?

You did great! Fear isn't something to be afraid of. It's a natural feeling in uncertain or dangerous situations. It helps us figure out what we need to do to overcome challenges. Fear is a helpful guide as we grow. You're not a coward, John."

John felt reassured and decided to keep learning through his fears.

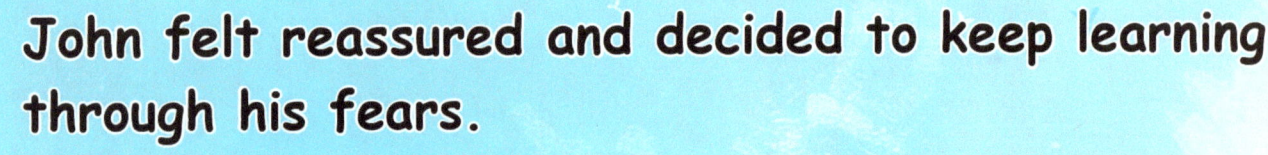

honglee books recommended books

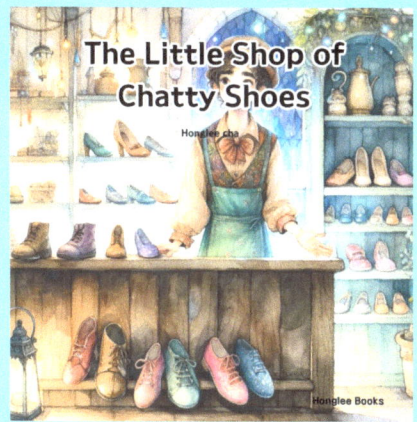
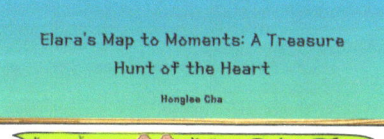

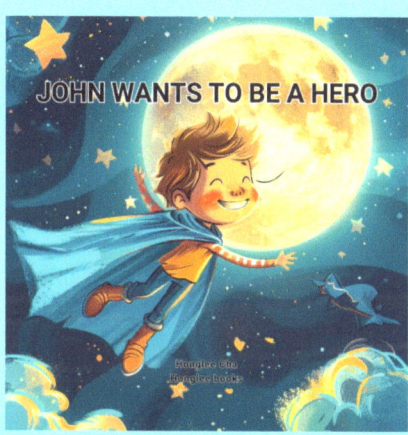

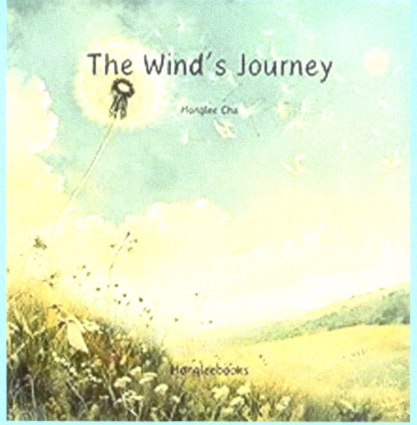
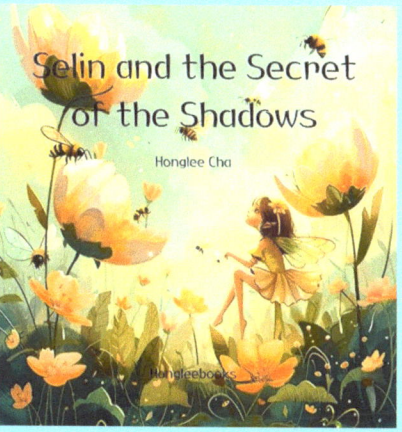

honglee books recommended books

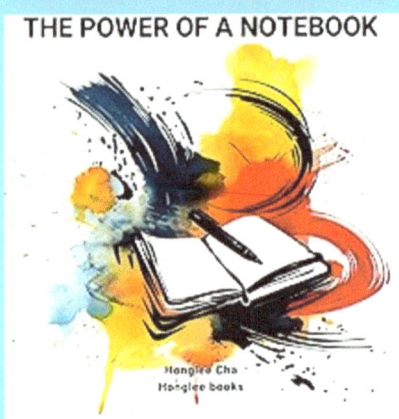
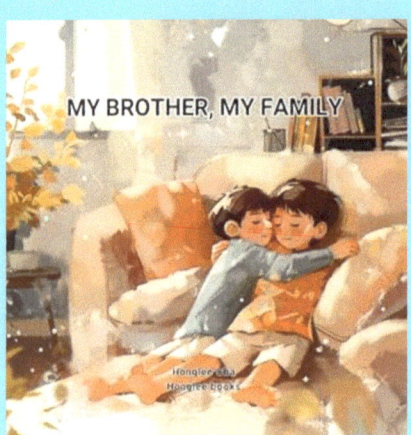
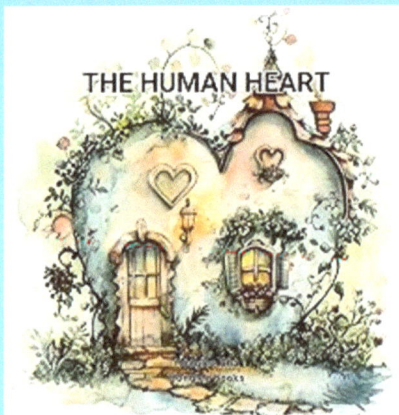

honglee books recommended series

john mystery story

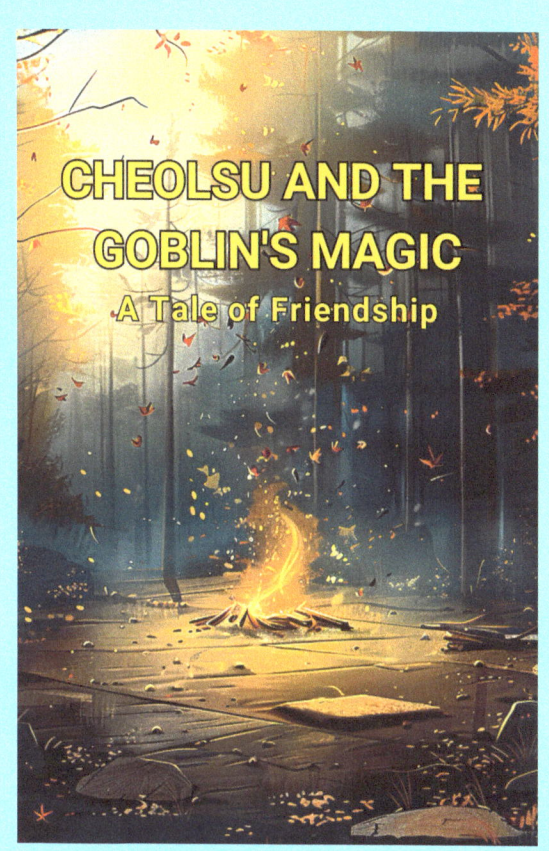

Cheolsu special story

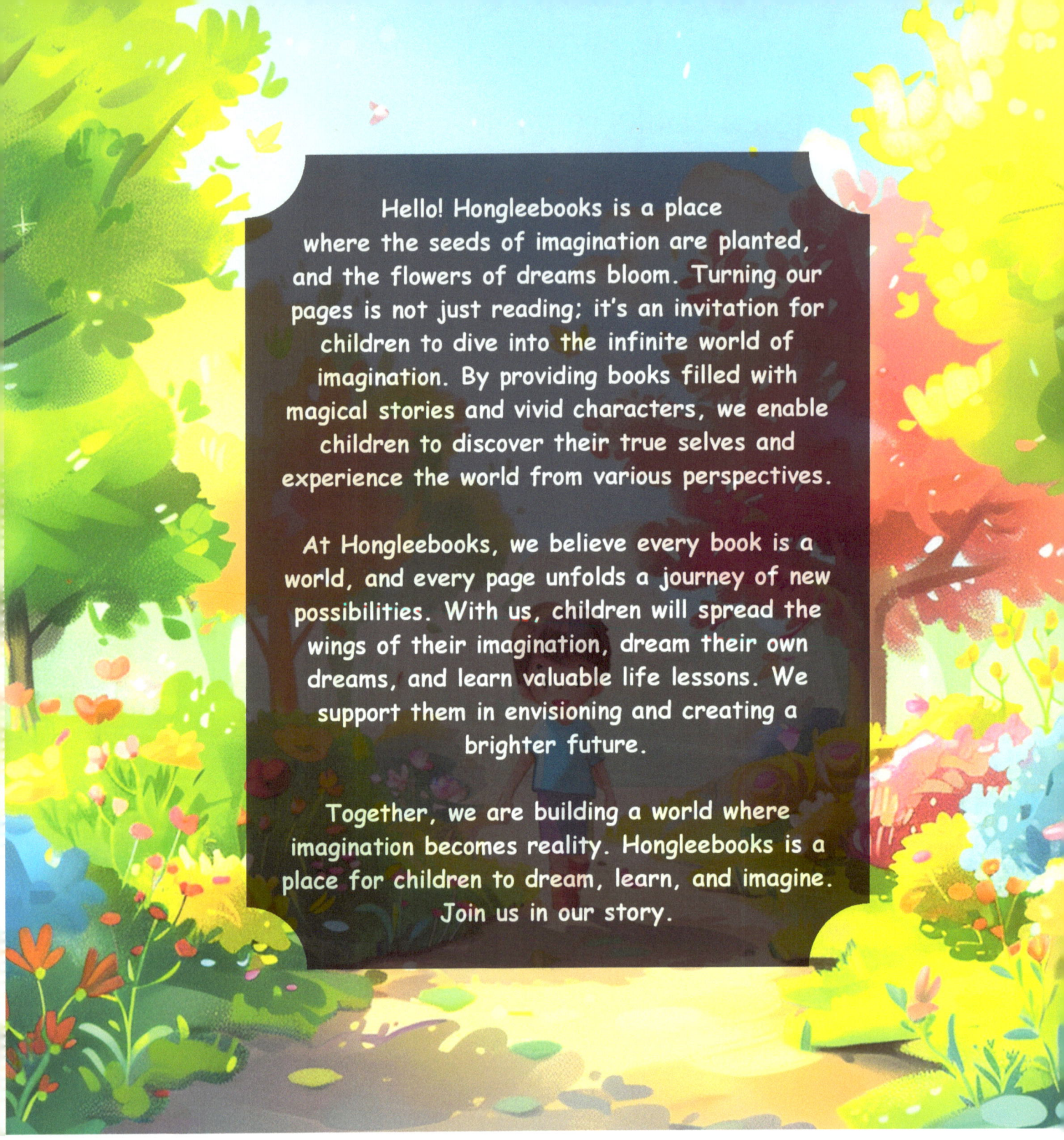

Hello! Hongleebooks is a place where the seeds of imagination are planted, and the flowers of dreams bloom. Turning our pages is not just reading; it's an invitation for children to dive into the infinite world of imagination. By providing books filled with magical stories and vivid characters, we enable children to discover their true selves and experience the world from various perspectives.

At Hongleebooks, we believe every book is a world, and every page unfolds a journey of new possibilities. With us, children will spread the wings of their imagination, dream their own dreams, and learn valuable life lessons. We support them in envisioning and creating a brighter future.

Together, we are building a world where imagination becomes reality. Hongleebooks is a place for children to dream, learn, and imagine. Join us in our story.

www.ingramcontent.com/pod-product-compliance
Lightning Source LLC
LaVergne TN
LVHW071701060526
838201LV00038B/402